THIS IS
BUSINESS

vol.1

The Ultimate Guide To Building Your Dream
Business Before College

Lamarr J Mann MBA

Forward

Have you ever encountered someone who was quiet, but you look into their eyes and you see an inferno blazing? I met Lamarr two years ago and after one conversation, I knew he was a man focused on making a positive change in the earth. I remember being in the midst of publishing my second book and as I shared my publishing journey with Lamarr, I could see his wheels turning.

Lamarr has a heart for helping people, especially young people tap into their God given potential and grow. In this work you will experience his heart, his intellect, and his passion. He has crafted a work that balances personal experience and knowledge, all coupled with practical instruction that speaks to all age levels. *This Is Business* is truly a work that will unlock the treasure of wealth that resides in each of us. If you desire to create a business and dream at a new level, do yourself a favor and read this book.

Dre Gleaton
Published Author/Blogger

Dedication

This book is dedicated to Robert Mann and Sharise Yancey. Mom and Dad, you are my heroes and I have always cherished every moment that I have with you. You created me with care, raised me to believe in God, and to have faith that all things are possible with God's grace. You worked hard to provide all the things I needed and even provided the "extras" as I grew up. I thank you for loving me unconditionally and supporting me through this game called "Life." You have helped me to become the man I am today and for that I am truly grateful. Finally, I dedicate this book to my future children. My hope is that you will one day read this book, be motivated, and inspired by every word to go after your dreams and make them tangible realities.

Prelude

A lot of young people simply don't understand business. As a young person, the earlier you can learn and enter the world of business; the faster you can turn a profit and begin building the life that you dreamed of. There are an endless number of things you can become or invent as a child or adult. There is no one set way to achieve your goals of having a business because businesses are varied and thus all require different focus points. If you are a teen, you might have heard about the many wonderful options that attending college affords you. You may be encouraged by your parents or family to enlist in the military when you graduate high school to assist you in launching into adulthood.

Now, what happens if you don't want to do any of that because it just doesn't feel right? College? You may not want to attend college right now and that is perfectly okay. With college level debt due to student loans being at an all-time high, yeah college may not be the plan for you. You also might have reservations about serving the duties required in the military. Or you might just want to be your own boss and own your own business. The reason why I wrote this book is because I wanted to help young aspiring entrepreneurs achieve their goals in both business and in life. If you think business is your thing, I wrote this book for teens like you.

There is a reason you are reading this book and thus the reason I am writing it. It is to help you uncover your skills and use those skills by applying them in the real world to create your version of business success. You are gifted, intelligent, a young individual of great talent, and resource. When you start a business at a young age you can help the economy by giving other people around you jobs. The same money you would need to own a nail salon, barbershop, or food truck would be the same money you would spend repaying loans for college. So, why not use that same money to fine tune your skills and start your business? Well, imagine being able to retire by the time your friends are really just starting their careers. Not only that, by starting a business you will also touch and change lives when you do it the right way. How incredible would that be for you?

As a young person, your life is virtually open to all the experiences the world has to offer. You have the power and potential to shape the world right now while you are a teenager, because teenagers know what the world needs. You are the expert or better yet the untapped resource. The owner of Facebook Mark Zuckerberg created what he felt his peers at Harvard wanted and now practically everyone in the world either has a Facebook page or knows someone who does. You are the expert and know what your friends want and need. Serve them. Mark knew that his friends needed a way to connect. He found a way to make that happen and now because of his resiliency and imagination he is worth over 72 billion dollars. If he would have waited, someone else would have created Facebook as we know it today.

The material and the examples in this book are dedicated to you because I have a passion for helping young people like yourself reach their dreams. When you look at your life and you see things are not going the way that you want them, you have to look at one person: yourself. How can you use your skills to create the better life that you want to live? When I thought about writing this book I thought about my future children. Even though I don't have any children right now. I know one day that I will and I would love for them to take over my businesses or even have their own. I want to help you! Yes, I'm talking to you, the person who is reading this right now. My wish is that you will dream big, reach for the stars, and remember that no matter what challenges you endure while pursuing your dreams, this is business.

Contents

This is Business, vol. 1

Lamarr J Mann, MBA

CHAPTER ONE

IT ALL STARTS WITH AN IDEA

Like A Boss

There are several reasons why you would want to start a business, but probably the most important or should I say most popular reason to start a business is to be your own BOSS. Nothing beats being able to create your own schedule. You determine the hours you want to work, the time you wake up to start your day, and what time you want to end your day. As the BOSS you have the flexibility to take a shorter or longer lunch break whenever you want to. As a business owner you are the BOSS and create the environment in which you want to work in. As the BOSS you control your professional future. I know firsthand that working for big companies your personal vision can get lost or even pushed to the side. In the corporate world you have meetings where you may have an idea or you may want to present something, but because of "fitting in" with the people in the room, you decide to keep quiet. However, it all changes when you own your business, because you have the ability to have your own ideas and push them forward. Your ideas will be the lifeline of your business.

Whenever you decide on an idea for your business, your name is on it, so at the end of the day there is no other type of job that provides control over your passion and ideas like owning your own business. Controlling your ideas and passion is so important because you are able to really make changes and truly help other people along the way. I believe that everybody wants to see something grow successfully. There is no greater feeling than seeing your idea be birthed, you watch it grow, and see it continue to build. This is one of the greatest personal benefits of having your own business, because it's a reminder of the potential and power that is inside of you to inject something great into the earth (through your business). I was able to see my mother's cleaning service start off as a one employee owned business and grow to a place where she was able to hire multiple employees over time. To grow her business we started with great service, a marketing plan, finance strategy, and also added a sales component which all working together were the gas in the engine that fueled the growth of her business.

There is no greater satisfaction than to witness your business begin to grow. It gives you so much confidence and positions you to be able to show sustained results and thus puts you in the room to network with the right people. As a young entrepreneur, having a business gives you the opportunity to experience mentorship. Mentorship is vital to the success and growth of your business. Having someone with business experience that you can go to for help and support helps ease the pressure that you will often feel as a budding business owner. Many mentors love to help younger entrepreneurs and the reason why is because they can see something in the young entrepreneur. Your potential and passion working together will always attract positive results and positive support.

Also, in business when you create a good brand and a good image that helps you as well because companies want to invest in companies that not only have a great product, but good branding as well. When we take a look at a particular burger restaurant and we see those golden arches we become inspired. Inspired to pull over, go through the drive-thru, or go inside to grab a quick bite to eat. The golden arches represents to us a fair food service and we are going to be able to get that pipping hot Double Cheeseburger along with those crisp hot fries. One other driver to owning your own business is the idea of consistent employment. Knowing that you will not be laid off by someone is also very empowering. In theory, whatever you want to do in your business you are able to do for the most part. You don't have to worry about a corporation telling you that they no longer need your services as long as you have customers or clients you will be able to sustain your business and live off of whatever results you get from it.

Lessons From The Busboy

I know it may seem like I am just some grown up guy who wanted to write a book about business but believe it or not I was at some point in time a teenager also. So, before we start you on your journey to becoming a young successful business owner, let me take you back to when I was 13. I wanted to have a job so bad so I could have extra money to buy clothes, cassettes, and hang out with my friends. I knew I was too young to go an apply for a job alone; so I asked my mom if I could get a permit from my middle school which would allow me to work. I got a job as a busboy at a local restaurant who specialized in serving breakfast food. I remember working hard on Saturday's and Sunday's eight hour shifts.

I spent my days greeting customers and wiping down tables. I worked with the waitstaff to make sure that I knew when the customers were leaving, so I could take the dishes to the washer and clean them. I would take the empty washer cart and do it all over again because this was my job and I was determined to do it well. I had to do all of this within sixty minutes (five minutes per table). The waitstaff would serve the customers, the customers would eat, and I would clean the tables. I kept my wash tub, gloves, and sanitation rag ready for action. I would clean those tables making sure there that no sugar, syrup, juice, or food remained on the table. I wanted to make sure that all those tables were not just clean, but clean clean within my sixty minute allotted timeframe. I worked hard and so fast that one of the waitresses had to tell me to slow down.

I wanted to make sure that the waitstaff could confidently sit another customer at any of the tables that I cleaned without complaints. Cleaning those tables was not only my job, but it was an important service that I provided to the restaurant. No one wants to sit down at a dirty table to eat a meal and if the table was not cleaned properly within a timely manner, the waitstaff's tips would suffer. Also, I would receive extra money from the staff throughout the day for my service. I repeated this for 6 ½ hours out my 8 hour shift- I had one hour lunch break and two 15 min breaks.

After two weeks of working my Saturday and Sunday schedule I finally received my first paycheck from the restaurant. I was so excited and to this day I still remember that first check like it was yesterday. It was exactly $105 and I thought this was the best thing that ever happened to me. It was the best thing that ever happened to me because I had support from my parents, I learned my duties for work, I performed my duties at work well, and I was paid for my performance. I took the $105 and purchased my 1st CD player and I was able to listen to music every day. On the flip side, what if I happened to own that restaurant? Can you imagine how big that first check would have been? As i sit here reminiscing on that first paycheck I also want to share with you a few things that I learned during my time as a busboy. I learned the following:

1. Don't take your opportunities for granted.

2. Always posture myself to be a learner.

3. I learned the importance of customer service which is key when dealing with people in general, but when you add in their food, great to good customer service is mandatory.

Activity One - Drafting The idea

In this chapter we covered, "what it takes" for you to develop an idea for your business. Use the questions listed below to assist you in drafting out your business idea.

1. What idea/passion do you have that you can turn into a business?

    _____

    _____

    _____

    _____

2. Summarize what is the goal of your business in one sentence.

    _____

    _____

    _____

    _____

Lamarr J Mann, MBA

CHAPTER TWO

TURN YOUR IDEAS INTO

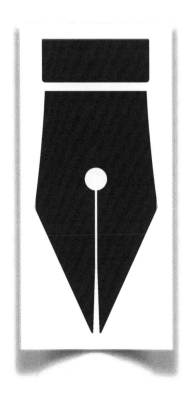

Not only do we need to have a good idea for a business, we need to have a strong plan. Having a plan will allow you to bring your vision to fruition. This chapter is dedicated to walking you through the necessary steps to help your business flourish. This world is filled with competition and things that will come your way. If you fail to plan, you plan to fail. Many individuals and companies who can give you money to fund your business will ask you what your business plan is. It will be the first question because it is the most important. Let's go over the steps you need to know in order to create a business plan for your company.

It has been said that "If you love what you do, then you will never work a day in your life." If this is the case, why not build a job around the things that you actually love? For example, one of my passions is real estate. The reason why I love real estate so much is because number one it helps families find homes. When I turned 17, I had an idea that I could own real estate. I liked the thought of buying a property or a place that I could potentially rent or even sell to another family to live in. I knew if I could provide a clean and affordable place for a family, then it would bring me a lot of joy. I was also excited at the thought of making money and being a landlord. I would sit in class and dream about owning commercial real estate. Buying a property one day and seeing my name on a shopping center or even buildings kept me dreaming.

I purchased my first home at 24. I thought to myself this is my golden opportunity to rent out my house and go through with my plans. During the time that I had my home I was able to successfully rent out my house and I was also able to repair and remodel things that needed to be fixed or changed in the home. I sat in my living room one day and realized what happened. I did it! I accomplished my dream of becoming a landlord. During this process, I lost money, I gained some money, but I learned a lot. Overall, I thought I made a nice profit by following my dreams. The question that you have to ask yourself is what do you really want to do when it comes to business, and how can it affect other people's lives? I knew I wanted to make this change in the world, and I had no fear when it came to the competition and hurdles that I had to overcome in order to turn my idea into a plan. **Your mindset about starting the business is important no matter the industry you want to go into.**

After I thought about what I needed to accomplish my dreams, the first thing I had to do was realize that I wanted to start a real estate business. So, of course I went through the beginning stages of the process to make my business official, this of course was the plan. I came up with a name for my business and at the time it was called "Destiny Business Enterprises." Destiny was a name that I always wanted to use as the name for my business because I understood that my destiny would be tied to not just starting a business, but a legacy. Next, I had to determine the type of property that I wanted to purchase (single-family or multi-family). A single-family unit is a building for one family vs. a multi-family unit known as a duplex or maybe even an apartment complex will have multiple families living in one building but individual units.

I was just starting out, I decided that I would only purchase one single-family unit, I would rent it out, and then I would at some point sell the unit for profit. The next step in the real estate business process that I had to tackle was finding the exact property that I wanted to purchase. To speed up this process I found a real estate agent that would help me locate the property I wanted to invest in, and to ensure that we were on the same page, I reviewed my goals with that particular agent. The agent and I located an area that I felt would be the best place for me to invest in and we found a place that I wanted to purchase in that area. At the time I may have put in three or four purchase offers and all of my offers got rejected.

What If The Plan Fails?

At that time I felt pretty down because I felt like this is my passion and this is something I really want to do. When you are making your plan it might not go as you would like, but it is no harm in making small changes to your plan. I thought that making a business 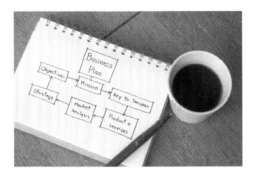 plan would be easy, so why is it so difficult for me to find the property of my dreams that I can make a profit off of? The agent also didn't seem to really understand what I wanted to do and that also gave me a little anxiety. It was at that time I decided to put my business in my own hands. There will be times like this when you will have to take the reins over the business that you want to build and put matters into your own hands. I started to find properties on my own and would contact my agent to meet in person to discuss the specific properties that I was asking her to search for. After three weeks of every day searching with my agent I finally found a property and we put an offer in and I got accepted. I was so ecstatic. I purchased my first property which needed minor improvements before I could move anyone in.

Remember, you are an important part of the plan because your first resource is you.

I had help from a subcontractor who did basic things to the unit such as painting walls, replacing outlets, changing door knobs, checking fixtures, and making sure the flooring and carpet were done right. It took roughly another 3 to 4 weeks before I could find a tenant to move into my property. In real estate you often can find a property manager who will manage the property for you and charge you a 10% to 15% fee depending on how you negotiate, I didn't want to pay 10 to 15% for a property manager so I decided to do property management on my own. I would say in business the more you can outsource your work, the better. I say this because you want to be able to search for other properties, be able to raise capital (money), and sometimes having to manage the property as well as other responsibilities can be troublesome. In this case I had to learn a business lesson the hard way. An example of what I mean is this, if you are the property management of your own property and let's say the toilet clogs up your tenant can now call you at any time day or night and ask you to be the person to unclog the toilet. Now, if I had a dedicated property manager I would not have had to get up to go and actually unclog a toilet or any other issues for that matter.

Some people are very handy. I happen not to be very handy so this was not the best situation for me. All and all I was able to move in a tenant, collect monthly rent, and have a paying tenant live in my home for almost two years. I had just finished my MBA and I decided to move back into my home and make it more of an office as I look for other opportunities in real estate and many years later, I was able to turn around and sell the property for a nice size profit. Thus, this real estate venture was not as bad as I thought it would be.

Let me pause here and ask you a very important question. "What do you think you want to do for your business?" Maybe you are good at cutting grass and you desire to start a landscaping business; or maybe you have an idea for fashion and you have a drive to go into the fashion world, or better yet you may have plans on becoming the next Mark Zuckerberg by founding an app or website like Facebook or even Instagram. Maybe you would like to partner with someone because you guys have the same idea and could be as simple as an ice cream stand. The bottom line is you have to decide where your passions are and figure out what you love most. I would say at the point you identify your passions you would do exactly what I was able to do when it came to Real Estate.

We will go into greater detail later in this book, but be sure that you have a passion for something. When I think about passion I think about something that you could do for the rest of your life regardless of how long it takes to complete the mission; but you would still be happy to do it anyway. For me, when it comes to real estate, it comes down to being able to help other people live the American dream of homeownership. You may want to feed the homeless, dress a client, or give a service that impacts the greater community at large. Think deep about the product or service that you would like to create or offer. When you think of services, you can think of things that people are really good at such as doing hair or nails. Someone may want to get a cosmetology license, open up a nail salon, or you could even be like my mother who had a cleaning service.

Built For Entrepreneurship

As you all know I've dedicated this book to my parents. My parents were both very hard workers. My father held down two jobs to make sure that my little brother and I had all that we needed and wanted during our school years. During this period of time, my mother being a hard worker herself, started a cleaning business from the ground up. I know my mother has a true passion for not just cleaning, but being a business owner. I remember being a junior in high school and my mother talking about entrepreneurship and it felt like a dream. My mother was so happy, she loved to gain new business, and loved all of the customers she had throughout that time. Thinking back to my high school years, I remember my mother talking about the fact that she had a cleaning service and I was in total awe.

I remember the very first time my mother took me to an office and said that it was an office that she was going to clean. She wanted me to help her and although she felt empowered, I also felt empowered because I knew that she had something different than someone who worked a traditional 9 to 5. I would always see a smile on her face when we walked into the industry store to purchase cleaning supplies. I mean she was smiling ear to ear as we purchased the different vacuums, brooms, mops, buckets, or anything related to her cleaning service. I felt like she had this special power and she knew that she had it as well. I also saw how happy her customers were as we walked into an office and we started cleaning. It didn't matter if it was simple dusting but after 45 minutes to an hour or so later to see the results of everything being sparkly clean, organized, and the customers being so happy and being proud. These were some of the things as a high school student that really shaped my desires of being an entrepreneur.

I just understood that there was something great about having the flexibility my mother had. She never missed anything because she always had the flexibility of changing her schedule for her jobs as needed. These are some of the things that some of my friends didn't have because their parents had to work numerous hours at a full-time job. My mother would have done anything for her customers and that was evident based on the type of effort she put into her work. She did work a lot of hours, but once again that smile of hers was always so bright. My mother was able to make very good money and in later chapters I'll talk more about how we were able to execute successful accounting, financing, marketing, and sales strategies for her business, but overall I want everyone who reads this book to be encouraged to find their passion and allow their passion to direct them to their pursuit of business.

Activity Two: "Who Will Be My Support System?"

As I explained earlier in this book, my mother has been a very important support system for me because she had her own business. Earlier we discussed the importance of mentorship to the success of young entrepreneurs (you). So with that being said, I would ask that as you read this work you begin to locate at least one to three people that you can consider your support system. It doesn't have to be someone who owns a business but you need somebody who you can trust and can discuss your goals with. You need someone who you can share your vision with and who is not afraid to provide you with constructive criticism. I would also say you need someone that is able to push and motivate you as well. Business in general can be very difficult , but it becomes even more difficult when you don't have the right support system in your corner.

So, don't be afraid to look for and pull on your support system when you are faced with challenges or you just need a simple nudge of motivation. Remember, this is an activity, so pause and take a few minutes to ask yourself and respond to the question, "who will be my support system as I become a young success business owner?" Don't forget to write down your responses. Identify at least one to three people that you can lean on for support as you begin your journey into entrepreneurship.

_____

_____

_____

_____

_____

_____

Activity Three: "What Does Success Mean To Me?"

Things change as you grow older but I would say in my teen years the most important thing to me was becoming a millionaire when I got older. The thought of being a millionaire was exciting to me from the age of thirteen to at least the age of nineteen. Now that I'm a little older, I no longer believe that success means being a millionaire; but I do believe that success for me is defined by my ability to help others. So, if only one person reads this book or if only one person starts a business from the nudge this book provides, I would feel as if I changed the entire world which is the greatest success for me. The reason why you have to define what success means to you is because it will be the force to push and drive you towards the goals you want to achieve.

Now, think hard about what success looks like to you and write it down. I would encourage you to come up with two successes that you can track and measure. And remember, by no means do you have to believe that money should be number one or even a part of your success list. Always understand that money will come as long as you have a great idea, work hard, and are selling a product or service the world needs. Money can sometimes lead to loss and unhappiness if not placed in the proper perspective. So again, take some time and write down two to three ideas of what you categorize as success.

_____

_____

_____

_____

_____

_____

_____

_____

_____

_____

_____

_____

Activity Four: The S.W.O.T. Analysis

SWOT [Strength.Weakness.Opportunities.Threats] - This acronym and term is very important in business. It helps you to understand the potential successes and or barriers of your business.

Let's get started here:

1.   Think about the idea you have for your company.

2.   Are there other businesses that are similar?

3.   How much do you know about your competition or the industry that you are trying to enter?

Write your answers here:

_____

_____

_____

_____

_____

_____

CHAPTER THREE

C . H . A . S . E .

(AS IN "CHASE YOUR DREAMS")

"A lot of people fail to prosper because they are
too busy dreaming in their sleep…"
- Edmond Mbiaka

You have a successful business plan mapped out but for some odd reason you refuse to follow it, you are setting yourself up to fall into a trap which could include legal challenges. Now, there are many people who are adults and way older than you or I, have graduated from college and they have no clue on how to successfully start a business. I went to college and I loved it! However, it was minimal help in my entrepreneurial drive. The classes did no more than put me in a place to be a wonderful *employee*. Anyone can earn a degree but it takes heart to run a business. A degree will help you get a job with a business where you are taught to work within a company for years. The aim of helping you start the business is the goal here, so I want to make sure that I help you start it right. Look at this chapter as your guide to the ideas you need to start your business.

There is A LOT that goes into starting your own company and it is my hope that the lessons in the next few chapters will simplify that process. To do so, we will do this by utilizing an easy to remember acronym: **C.H.A.S.E** (as in "**chase** your dreams")

C is for **choose**. You apply choose by making the decision on the type of product, service, or skill you would like to offer. If you have your plan together from chapter 2, you have already decided on this step.

H is for **have your paperwork together**. When you begin sharing your business idea with people, you also need to have your ideas documented, and also have the documents needed to officially establish your business. The *have* is about preparation.

A is for **ask**. Don't be afraid to ask for help. Your friends, parents, and support system are all available resources to you. They may have connections to people who can help you begin.

S is for **sell**. Being in business is about helping the world in some way but it is also about making money. Always remember that sales equal money and money equals successful business growth. So, no sells, equals no business revenue.

E is for **enjoy the ride.** No matter what you do, the journey will get tough at times, so enjoy the process of building something that you know will last.

Documents Matter

Now that we have an outline of some sort, let's start with making sure your business documents are in order. One of the first things you need to do is register the name of your business with the Secretary of State for your location. Check with your individual state for guidelines to do this. Once you go to the Secretary of State's website you should see a section for corporations. If you don't, search the website to find out how to start a business. If you need help, you can always contact the number on the website. Always remember to check that the website ends in ".gov". Some other websites might be out there but they are counterfeits and not official resources for business.

Get Ready! Get Ready!

Once you have your plans together and are ready to start, you will have to pay a fee to legally register your business. Do not worry about this because it normally is money that you can raise easily or get from family or friends. Once you officially register your business, the real work now begins. So, GET READY! Follow these steps below but always keep your plan in mind.

- Comply With Licensing and Zoning Laws

- Conduct a Business Name Search

- Name a Registered Agent

- Draft Articles of Incorporation

- Explain Articles of Incorporation

- File Articles of Incorporation With the State

- Write up Corporate Bylaws

- Start a Corporate Records Book

- Hold Your First Board Meeting

Remember that you have an amazing vision, but you have to have a plan to in order to make the vision come alive.

The Main Business Types

There are 3 main types of business. LLC or Limited Liability Company, Sole Proprietorship, or a Corporation. The most common business is the LLC and many start out registering their company as this type of business for several reasons. It protects you from getting sued personally and having someone take all of your stuff; and the normal time it takes to incorporate your business would be one to six weeks. The cost is around $100 to $500, depending on where your company is located or if it is online. **DO NOT MAKE THIS HARDER THAN WHAT IT SHOULD BE.** And say this out loud: "I will not let fear or my lack of knowledge stop me from starting my company.

The incorporation is regulated at the state and city level, so with the help of your parents you can read up on local requirements. Whenever you need local or state-specific help, always be sure to seek counsel from a lawyer. . Corporations must have an EIN which is **[Employer Identification Number]**which is completely free on the IRS website. This is important because it is like a social security number for your business.

You want to open a business bank account *after* you have set up the Articles of Incorporation and received your EIN. You want to make sure to keep personal and business finances separate. You want to search for banks that may offer bonuses for opening up a business account. You want to make sure you sit down with the business banker and tell them more

about yourself and the business you have. When you build a great relationship with your bank you open opportunities for financing which we will discuss later in the book.

The Checklist:

1. **My Business Name is**_____

2. **I registered my business with the Secretary of State on** _____

3. **I registered my business as a (see main business types)**_____

4. **The EIN number for my business is**_____

5. **I have established a business bank account under my business name of** _____

6. **My business account number is** _____

7. **My line of credit for this account is** _____

CHAPTER FOUR

WHOSE BUYING YOUR STUFF?

(THE MARKETING OF IT ALL)

"Good marketing makes the company look smart.
Great marketing makes the customer feel smart."
– Joe Chernov

The first thing you should know about brand marketing is it has almost nothing to do with your favorite colors, logo, and funny catch phrase to sell your business. It has everything to do with your ideal customer, how they think, what they like, and also how well you will treat them. This part of the book will discuss (of course logos and branding) but it will also help you to understand the science behind getting your business out to the public. However, before you make your first sale you need to know where your ideal customer is and how to find them.

Let's think about a scenario that shows how you market through your company. You head to your favorite fast food restaurant, ready to order a meal. You are very hungry and have the exact amount to pay with. You walk in with a great attitude because you know you will catch a movie afterwards. After waiting in line for 5 to 10 minutes, you are next in line. The cashier asks "How many I help you?" (with an attitude) and you politely say "I would like to get the double-stacked burger value meal." The cashier then says, "Can you repeat that again? I couldn't hear you." You notice that when she says that she's laughing with her coworker and she's paying no attention to you. You politely tell the cashier again "I would like a number two double-stacked burger value meal and can you please remove the pickles from my sandwich." Once more, the cashier says you said "you want pickles," and you see that she's playing with her coworker and not paying attention to you. Then, you say for the third time "I Want A Double-Stacked Burger Value Meal!" At this point you're upset by the fact that this cashier is not listening to you and you had a great day and everything was going well until you walked right in front of her.

Next up, you pay with cash and the cashier does not give you the correct change back. Once again you're annoyed and you tell the cashier I was supposed to get $14.59. Do you want to give me the $.59 back? The cashier laughs and says "my bad" and gives you the $.59 that she should have given you the first time. So after all of these events, you drive off. While riding to the movies, you decide that you're going to bite into your stacked burger without pickles and before you bite, something tells you to check underneath the bun before you do. And guess what? You see pickles! Now you are upset and you don't have enough time to go back to the restaurant because you've driven away. Now, you have to meet somebody for the movies and you're frustrated because you're allergic to pickles. The question is how do you feel when you receive service like this? Do you feel like going back to the same place? Does this restaurant still remain at the top of your favorite restaurants list?

This entire situation is marketing and sales wrapped all into one and from it we can pull out three important learning nuggets:

1. You only get one shot to please the customer

2. Once the customer does not feel good, they will let others know about the situation.

3. Your business is your brand.

The reason these questions and the situation are so important is because as a young business owner you have to make sure that you satisfy all of your customers and clients with excellence. Make excellence your brand because that is what your customers will remember you for. Let's break this down. Your marketing starts the moment your customer encounters you. Actually before they meet you, whatever you or a former customer has put out into the universe is what they will remember about you.

Think of your favorite place to eat? What are the top three things you love about them?

1. _____

2. _____

3. _____

I can almost guarantee the things you love comes from a direct marketing strategy that the company has in place. You are your marketing strategy when you are first starting a business. This is very important to keep in mind.

When I think back to my mother's cleaning service I think about the fact that one of her mottos was "the job always has to be good and the customer has to be happy". There will be times when we would complete an office knowing it was sparkling clean, and maybe receive an email or even a phone call from the operations manager even the secretary for the office. Normally when an operations manager or the secretary calls you it's for two reasons: 1) You've done a great job or 2) There is something they want you to come back and fix. In all of the years that I've worked with my mother, I've never witnessed her ever tell a customer that she was not going back. She always made sure that she had process in place for her customers needs to get addressed. My mother would always make sure the needs of her customers were met because she understood the impact of word-of-mouth to her business. Word of mouth is going to be critical to the success and longevity of your business. As a matter of fact if the customer goes to friends or family and says that the product or service that you offer as a new business owner is not good then it can potentially derail your business. On the flip side of course if the service is great it can impact your business in a positive way.

The next thing you have to think about is the impact of the Internet and social media, if your customer is not satisfied with the product or service and they make a review on a website or app it can last forever. Think about it. When trying to purchase something online, I'm looking for reviews. I always check the reviews to make sure that I am going to a great restaurant or the product that I want to purchase is in good standing with other customers. If I wanted to buy a vehicle from a specific car dealership and I see that they have a two star rating on a five star scale with five being the best, I would never buy my vehicle from there. Now that's not to say that sometimes customers can give you a bad review even when the service or product is great but for the most part, "the customer is always right." The best thing to do in the situation is to make sure that you have a great communication strategy. Whether it be through text, phone, or email; communication with your customer or client to make sure they're completely satisfied is a non-negotiable.

The last item you want to look at is the customer's potential to either help you gain more business or stop you from getting more business. So in the case of my mother's cleaning service, if someone loved her services from day one they would go to their friends, family, and colleagues to say what a great service they received. The customer can also say at first I didn't believe that the service was done to my liking but they came back to clean the area that I felt wasn't clean and we got an agreement that the service was done correctly. That goes along way when it comes down to it. So, always have integrity when it comes to making sure that you satisfy your customers to the fullest extent.

Here is a quick marketing plan example (Layla's Lemonade Stand):

The goal of a marketing plan is to look at where you want to be in the future. What is your company's marketing strategy; work with your team. The first thing that Layla needs to do is **create a marketing plan!**

The Plan

A marketing plan consists of 2 parts:

1. A summary of your marketing goals and objectives, your marketplace

2. The tactics required to achieve your marketing strategy.

Customer Strategy and Relationships

Once your business is up and running, you need to start attracting clients and customers. You'll want to start with the basics by writing a unique selling proposition (USP) and creating a marketing plan. Then, explore as many small business marketing ideas as possible so you can decide how to promote your business most effectively.

Once you have completed these business start-up activities, you will have the most important bases covered. Keep in mind that success doesn't happen overnight, but use the plan you've created to consistently work on your business, and you will increase your chances of success.

Marketing Research - Drives a better understanding of customer behavior and buying patterns.

Layla would start by identifying competition. Identify who your competitors are and how you can be different. Use Google for this. Ideally Layla should research top lemonade stands in the city or look at the lemonade stands in the states. She would look at least five different companies and what makes them stand out. Layla would then need to examine her company to see what can make it better in comparison to similar companies in your area. Depending on the type of business you are starting, you can use Instagram to also see what types of business are out there. Also, do not forget the library! There are so many books (outside of the one you are reading) that will give you information on how to start your company.

After you learn about your particular business, you want to look at who you are selling to and how you can sell to them. Create your ideal customer in your mind. How old are they, what are the demographics of the customer you have in mind? What areas do they live in? What other stores do they shop at? You should know your customer's demographics including age, gender, occupation, lifestyle, and buying trends. It may sound silly to create a fake ideal customer avatar, but it is so important that Layla understands these things about this person so that she can market to them. She should also know the following:

- Who will benefit from your products/services?

- What companies offer similar products/services now?

- What is the competition?

Marketing Plan Strategies - Advertising, Direct marketing, trade shows (All the things that create your favorable business image) again the strategies should be simple, and in Layla's case she might just use a sign in her parent's front yard. This is a very simple marketing strategy at best.

Marketing Plan Budget - How much money do you have to achieve your goals? Well, fortunately for you lots of marketing is free because you have social media to give your free advertisement. You may want to do other things to promote your company, but starting it is free. That is a good thing. Remember that word of mouth will carry you far so ask your new customers to share the word.

Marketing Goals - Your goals will be based on how you plan to grow your business. You will set your goals based on how much you want to increase in sales.

Marketing Mix (4P's of Marketing) – Place, Price, Promotion, and place. This is something simple that all people can remember. If you have a business that is in the wrong place, then you cannot sell. If Layla wants to sell her lemonade to teenagers, but her neighborhood only has adults then she would need to find where teenagers hang out and advertise to them.

Price is important because if your competitor is four dollars and yours is six dollars then what is the reason that your lemonade is higher? Do you have better ingredients? You have to know what gives you a competitive edge.

Promotion - If nobody knows about your product or service, then how can your product sell?

Product - Create quality products and nobody will forget you. Give bad quality service or products and everyone will not forgive you. Very simple to remember.

Monitoring of Marketing Results - Did the marketing plan I put in place work? What can I change?

Market Penetration - Driving Sales

When I was in the 3rd grade my family decided to move from a house in a bad neighborhood to an apartment in a better neighborhood. We were moving also because my little brother would be joining our family later in the year. We were so excited to be moving to another place where violent crimes decreased. I was happy that my little brother was on the way and we would be in a better space. I was happy but nervous that I would be attending a new school in a new district. What are the things that most people do when they move is either take all of the stuff that they have acquired over time with them or they let certain things go. In this case, we wanted to get rid of some of the old items that we had so when we moved into a new place we would get new furniture, new clothes, etc. My family decided to have a garage sale, and I was so happy about that. The reason why was of course because we could make a little extra cash by selling old items. I realize that the extra cash could help with buying new items for our new apartment and also just the thought of having some cash made me happy. So we got posters and markers from the store so we could "market" and post "Please come to our garage sale on X Street."

The week before the garage sale I was so excited that we were selecting the items that were going to be used for the garage sale and that we actually were writing everything out on the posters. I felt like this was going to attract so many customers. The garage sale was taking place at my mother's friend's house and we had to set all of the items up and wait for everyone to come. I remember the night before the garage sale I was so excited. I was anxious because I just couldn't wait to meet some of the customers that would come to the garage sale. I had thoughts in my head about what I would say to potential customers. I was thinking about the fact that we had a jar where people could place tips or even just pay for the items I even thought about pricing for some of the items. Some of the items that were listed were living room items, dining room items, mom and dad's clothes, and even some of my own clothes.

Then the big day came, I remember it like it was yesterday. We got up early because the garage sale started at 8 AM. We planned for at least a week to have our marketing posters up. My mother and I were there from 8 AM to at least 3 PM. Only two people showed the whole day and unfortunately those two people didn't purchase anything. I felt devastated. I couldn't comprehend how we had great products, we posted several posters on different street corners like, we were on time, we had a good game plan, and only two people showed up and no one bought anything. I felt bad for my family because once again I felt like we could use some of this money for other household items and we came up short because we couldn't sell anything. So we took most of the items and donated them to either the Goodwill or Salvation Army. In retrospect it may have been best that we donated the majority to charity because someone was able to benefit from the items that we had.

Garage Sale Lessons:

With an understanding of business and how having a successfully executed marketing plan would have led to increased sales flow, when I think about that garage sale, there of course would be a few things that I would've changed The first thing to remember is anytime you have a great product or service you must give the customer or the client time to understand the brand that you're actually pushing out there. It takes numerous days, weeks, or even months to make sure that you have a great marketing campaign in place. The more customers you touch, the better chance you have with customers understanding what you're trying to sell. After analyzing my garage sale for example, here are the adjustments that I would have made:

1. Made sure that people know the garage sale was on September 1.

2. Started my marketing campaign thirty days prior on August 1.

3. Started marketing to friends, family, and coworkers at my job etc.

   - The reason why you want to make sure that your family, your friends, coworkers, and people that know you know about your efforts is because it is a great way to receive free marketing people which is called **"word of mouth."**

4. I would have purchased my posters and markers earlier.

5. I would have posted posters in more areas to drive increased market penetration.

6. Added contact information (phone number or even email address) so potential customers can contact us to ask questions.

- Today we have internet, social media, and a multitude of digital storefronts such as Amazon and eBay that I would definitely use if I had a garage sale in this day and age.

7. I would've had two different garage sales one on September 1 and maybe an encore or follow up the next week. (**Lesson** - give your customers and clients enough time to view the items your selling and also provide them with enough time to make informed decisions).

As I look back, those two customers came to the garage sale with the intentions of purchasing something, but probably walked away because pricing was too high. In sales, you have to ensure that you have both great selling and negotiation skills. Of course we're in business to make money so we can't give away items for free, but we need to make sure that we're meeting customers halfway when it comes down to negotiation. Now is the best time for young business owners to go into any industry whether it be selling online or selling in person because the resources available don't require you to leave your home to be successful.

In terms of marketing and sales you have to make sure that you understand how much it costs for your marketing materials. The honest reality that can learn from the garage sale is that it doesn't cost a lot to sell items, but your presentation of what you're selling is important. One must make sure that the items presented look sharp and are visible for people view them in their best light possible.

Thanks to the internet and social media we no longer have to sit in front of a store or post signs on telephone poles, we can now market from the privacy of our own homes. You can post your items on various selling apps or websites and have the ability to reach people all over the United States, and in some cases, throughout the world. In the event you have the same results that I had during my garage, please never give up. Remember, if it doesn't go right the first time, go back to the drawing board, correct your plan, and try again.

Sales Plan

A sales plan is a strategy that sets out sales targets and identifies the steps you will take to meet your targets. A sales plan will help you accomplish the following:

- **Define** a set of **sales targets** for your business.

- **Choose sales strategies** that are suited to your target market.

- **Identify sales tactics** for your sales team

- **Activate, motivate** and **focus** your **sales team**

- **Budget and clarify steps** you'll take to achieve your targets

- **Review** your **goals** periodically and improve your approaches to sales.

- A **sales plan sits within,** or **alongside,** a **marketing plan** to direct the efforts of your sales team.

This may seem like a lot at first but everything you do in business should have a strategy. When you sell items you want to think about how you are going to sell your items. Basically, how can you make the most money from items by doing the least amount of work. Again, sales are based on the service. Once you decide what you will sell if it is good enough, it will essentially sell itself. Yes marketing plans will be needed, but ultimately it boils down to the term I learned in my economics class called "supply and demand". What kind of things do you supply to the consumer and how much do they want it.

This guide explains the importance of having a sales plan, helping you develop, implement, and review your business's sales plan. The first step of writing a USP (unique selling proposition) requires that you take a step back and review the basics included in your mission statement, business plan, market analysis, and overall business goals. Start by answering some preliminary questions that recap what your business is selling, who you're selling to, and why you are selling your specific product or service.

For example, a company that sells moving boxes may compile and answer questions like this:

- **What products or services are you selling?** - Boxes and moving supplies.

- **Who is your target audience?** - Local homeowners who are moving and don't have a lot of time to look for used boxes in order to pack.

- **What does your business do well?** - We provide quick, responsive service while making the purchasing process easy for our customers.

- **What is your most important customer-focused business goal?** - Helping our customers get the moving supplies they need quickly, easily, and affordably.

Activity Five - Developing Your USP (Unique Selling Proposition)

In order to sell a successful product, you must have a solid sells strategy. This activity is focused on helping you develop your USP. Think about the product or service that you selling and once you have a clear picture of it, answer the question listed below. The answer to these questions will become the rough draft for your USP. If you get stuck, refer back to pages 31-32 for assistance.

1. What products or services are you selling?

_____

_____

2. Who is your target audience?

_____

_____

_____

3. What does your business do well?

_____

_____

_____

4. What is your most important customer-focused business goal?

_____

_____

_____

CHAPTER FIVE

IT TAKES MONEY TO MAKE MONEY - HOW MUCH DO YOU NEED TO START A BUSINESS?

"You can't have a million-dollar dream with a minimum-wage work ethic."
– Stephen C. Hogan

Lamarr J Mann, MBA

Take a moment to visualize yourself writing a check from your business to you. Imagine how good it would feel to walk into a bank and cash a check from a company that you created. That is one of the benefits of running your own company. But wait...before you can make money you have to figure out how to start the company of your dreams without financial help.

Sure, your dad might be a millionaire, or your mom can help you buy a few items, or connect you with resources for your company; but what if they can't? In this chapter, we will discuss ways that you can get money to start your business. And spoiler alert: It might be way easier than you think.

The most important part to starting and running a successful business is finance. Do you know the amount of funds you need to start a business can be as little as $250? You may say to yourself now, that's great but how in the world can you start my business with $250. Great question!!! You have to remember that as long as you are following the set up steps provided from the previous chapters, your business has started. You will now need to look deeper into the type of business you have and this is where you may need money. The key to finance is to do as much of the ground work as possible yourself. As I think about the cleaning business from a financial perspective, you would need to consider the particular cost associated to start this business.

You want to open a business bank account once you have setup the articles of Incorporation and received your EIN. You want to make sure you keep personal and business finances separate. You want to search for banks that may offer bonuses for opening up a business account. You want to make sure you sit down with the business banker and tell them you're more about yourself and the business you have. When you build a great relationship with your bank you open opportunities for financing which we will discuss later in the book,, but here are a few banks you can consider would include:

- Local Credit Union

- Wells Fargo

- SunTrust Bank

- Chase Bank

Financial Planning

Put together a spreadsheet that estimates the one-time startup costs for your business (licenses and permits, equipment, legal fees, insurance, branding, market research, inventory, trademarking, grand opening events, property leases, etc.), as well as the amount of money you anticipate that you will need to keep your business running for at least 12 months (rent, utilities, marketing and advertising, production, supplies, travel expenses, employee salaries, your own salary, etc.). Those numbers combined will determine the initial investment you will need to launch your business. Now that you have a rough number in mind, there are a number of ways you can fund your small business which include:

- Financing

- Small business loans

- Small business grants

- Angel investors

- Crowdfunding

Accounting

Keeping good records is one of the most important aspects of maintaining and growing your business. Small businesses run most effectively when there are systems in place. One of the most important systems for a small business is an accounting system. Your accounting system is necessary in order to create and manage your budget, set your rates and prices, conduct business with others, and file your taxes. You can set up your accounting system yourself, or hire an accountant to take away some of the guesswork.

If you decide to get started on your own, you may consider Quicken, Xero, & Sage which are three of top accounting software options available today. If you decided to go another route, you should consider these vital questions when choosing your software.

1. What is working with my current accounting process?

2. What is not working with my current account process?

3. What type of business do I have?

4. Where do I want my business to grow in one year? Three Years? Five Years and beyond?

5. What features do I absolutely need from an accounting software?

6. Which features would I like to have if possible?

7. How much am I willing to spend on accounting software?

8. Do I want a cloud-based service or locally installed on a single computer/laptop?

Final Activity - It Takes Money To Make Money

After reading this chapter you should have a solid understanding that money fuels your business and also provides insight into the success of your business. In this exercise, I want you focus on the accounting aspects of your business and answer the question listed below.

1. **How will you fund your startup business?**

    _____

    _____

    _____

2. **What expenses will you incur starting up your business?**

    _____

    _____

    _____

3. What does A - L = OE mean to you?

_____

_____

_____

4. What actions will you take to keep your assets high?

_____

_____

_____

Lamarr J Mann, MBA

CLOSING

THIS IS BUSINESS VOL. 1

In the beginning of this book I stated one of the major reasons that many strive to be a business owner is the idea of being boss. Now that you made it to the end of the first volume of This is Business, I want to help you bring everything together and to that let me elaborate on what it means to be a boss. Being a boss is more complex than not having someone telling you what to do. It is more detailed than just paying yourself? Being a boss means that every decision that you make for or about your business, falls squarely on your shoulders. This means if make a horrible business decision, there is no one to blame and no one to fix the mistake but you, most times. I say most times, because remember you have a support system that you can lean on for advice, direction, and sometime they will even help you clean up your mistakes.

One of the greatest qualities of boss is their ability to be a self-starter. Being a self-starter means that you don't wait for someone else to tell you do something, you do it because you know that it needs to be done. To be a self-starter means that you must also be motivated. To a boss in any industry you must also have a fire burning within yourself that drives your motivation and that thing is passion. Passion is not something that someone else can give you or something that you can pay for, passion starts within. As you read these words, I want to remind you that you have the passion to be successful. How do I know? I know that you have passion, because you opened and read a book titled, This is Business, Vol.1. Also, bosses look at ways that they can positively impact the lives of those close to them and the world.

As boss, I often think about those families in the world who may not have financial stability so becoming a young entrepreneur can help families in their time of need. I think about the positive impact that businesses can have on my family and I. What better way than to have the young generation start as early as possible?

There is a certain element to working with other people. I know how important a business can be in shaping the life you get to live. Your goal is to give back to the world. That's my passion and the main reason I wrote this book. We have an alarming rate of youth today who have succumb to the pressure of society because of what they feel they should do based upon what others are doing. Don't get stuck in this cycle. You were created for a purpose and were set apart with a gift and a skill set. If I could go back and be 14 years old again, and read this very book

I'd be a lot more successful than I am today. I have been afforded the opportunity to travel the world at the expense of the companies I work for, but my biggest pay day has been my ability to control my own business. Ideas are the skeleton of the business but it means nothing without the work.

After reading this book my hope is that you have found a step by step guide to assist you in uncovering and applying skills that will pay you later. Remember, It's much better to write yourself a check than to wait on a company to pay you every two weeks or once a month. If this work planted a seed and becomes the water that helps you start a business, that means I have done my part. I was in it and I have seen the ups and downs. I realized that sometimes your business has a season, so you might not be doing this forever. You might have a great business for 5 years, be okay with making money and never running the same business again, but having the experience to launch another one that is even more successful than the last. Experience in business is priceless, but if invested right, you will receive a maximum return. Remember, "your business will work when your work is effortlessly your passion" because this is business.

Lamarr J Mann, MBA

Appendix

ACTIVITIES, GLOSSARY, & MORI

Activity One - Drafting The idea

In this chapter we covered, "what it takes" for you to develop an idea for your business. Use the questions listed below to assist you in drafting out your business idea.

1. What idea/passion do you have that you can turn into a business?

    _____

    _____

    _____

    _____

2. Summarize what is the goal of your business in one sentence.

    _____

    _____

    _____

    _____

Activity Two: "Who will be my support system?"

As I explained earlier in this book, my mother has been a very important support system for me because she had her own business. Earlier we discussed the importance of mentorship to the success of young entrepreneurs (you). So with that being said, I would ask that as you read this work you begin to locate at least one to three people that you can consider your support system. It doesn't have to be someone who owns a business but you need somebody who you can trust and can discuss your goals with. You need someone who you can share your vision with and who is not afraid to provide you with constructive criticism. I would also say you need someone that is able to push and motivate you as well. Business in general can be very difficult , but it becomes even more difficult when you don't have the right support system in your corner.

So, don't be afraid to look for and pull on your support system when you are faced with challenges or

you just need a simple nudge of motivation.
Remember, this is an activity, so pause and take a few
minutes to ask yourself and respond to the question,
"who will be my support system as I become a young
success business owner?" Don't forget to write down
your responses. Identify at least one to three people
that you can lean on for support as you begin your
journey into entrepreneurship.

_____

_____

_____

_____

_____

_____

_____

_____

_____

_____

Activity Three: "What Does Success Mean To Me?"

Things change as you grow older but I would say in my teen years the most important thing to me was becoming a millionaire when I got older. The thought of being a millionaire was exciting to me from the age of thirteen to at least the age of nineteen. Now that I'm a little older, I no longer believe that success means being a millionaire; but I do believe that success for me is defined by my ability to help others. So, if only one person reads this book or if only one person starts a business from the nudge this book provides, I would feel as if I changed the entire world which is the greatest success for me. The reason why you have to define what success means to you is because it will be the force to push and drive you towards the goals you want to achieve.

Now, think hard about what success looks like to you and write it down. I would encourage you to come up with two successes that you can track and measure. And remember, by no means do you have to believe that money should be number one or even a part of your success list. Always understand that money will come as long as you have a great idea, work hard, and are selling a product or service the world needs. Money can sometimes lead to loss and unhappiness if not placed in the proper perspective. So again, take some time and write down two to three ideas of what you categorize as success.

_____

_____

_____

_____

_____

_____

_____

_____

_____

_____

Activity Four: The S.W.O.T. Analysis

SWOT [Strength.Weakness.Opportunities.Threats] -
This acronym and term is very important in business.
It helps you to understand the potential successes and
or barriers of your business.

Let's get started here:

1. Think about the idea you have for your company.

2. Are there other businesses that are similar?

3. How much do you know about your competition
    or the industry that you are trying to enter?

Write your answers here:

_____

_____

_____

_____

_____

_____

Activity Five - Developing Your USP (Unique Selling Proposition)

In order to sell a successful product, you must have a solid sells strategy. This activity is focused on helping you develop your USP. Think about the product or service that you selling and once you have a clear picture of it, answer the question listed below. The answer to these questions will become the rough draft for your USP. If you get stuck, refer back to pages 31-32 for assistance.

1. **What products or services are you selling?**

   _____

   _____

2. **Who is your target audience?**

   _____

   _____

   _____

3. What does your business do well?

_____

_____

_____

4. What is your most important customer-focused business goal?

_____

_____

_____

Final Activity - It Takes Money To Make Money

After reading this chapter you should have a solid understanding that money fuels your business and also provides insight into the success of your business. In this exercise, I want you focus on the accounting aspects of your business and answer the question listed below.

1. How will you fund your startup business?

_____

_____

_____

_____

2. What expenses will you incur starting up your business?

_____

_____

_____

_____

3. What does A - L = OE mean to you?

_____

_____

_____

_____

4. What actions will you take to keep your assets high?

_____

_____

_____

_____

Glossary

Accounts Payable (AP): Accounts payable are amounts owed by the business to vendors, suppliers, landlords, and other service providers. These are recorded as a liability on the balance sheet.

Accounts Receivable (AR): Accounts receivable are amounts of money owed to the business by customers or clients for goods and services rendered. Because the clients have a legal obligation to pay, the amounts are entered as an asset on the balance sheet.

Accruals: Accruals are revenues that are earned but not yet formally entered into the books (such as completed but not invoiced sales) or expenses that are incoming but not received (such as goods purchased but not yet invoiced).

Assets: Assets are anything of monetary value owned by the business. Typical tangible business assets include land, buildings, equipment, cash, vehicles, accounts receivable, etc. Intangible assets include client lists, franchise agreements, favorable finance or lease agreements, brand names, patents, copyrights, etc. Assets are expressed in terms of their cash value on balance sheets.

Bad Debt Expense: Bad debts are incurred when customers do not pay amounts owed. They are recorded as an expense on financial statements.

Balance Sheet: A balance sheet is a snapshot of a company's financial status at a particular point in time. It is organized into two main columns, with assets in one column and liabilities and equity in the other. The two sides always equal each other (in other words, assets = equity minus liabilities).

Capital (Also Known as Working Capital): Working capital is money that a company has available to pay bills or reinvest. It is equal to the value of all current assets minus current liabilities and is considered a key measure of the health of a business.

Cash Flow Statement: The cash flow statement shows the movements of cash and cash equivalents in and out of the business. The cash flow statement is an important tool for evaluating business health, as it's possible to show a profit on the income statement while draining cash from the business. Most companies that fail do so due to chronic cash flow problems.

Depreciation: Depreciation occurs as business assets such as vehicles and equipment decline in value over time due to use or obsolescence. Depreciation is an important tax deduction—a percentage of the original value of the asset can be written off every year based on the rate of depreciation.

Dividends: Dividends are distributions of a portion of company earnings to owners (shareholders) of the business. Dividends can be issued on a regular or non-regular basis and may consist of cash or additional shares in the business. For tax purposes, a business owner may prefer dividends to salary.

Entrepreneur: A person who organizes and operates a business or businesses, taking on greater than normal financial risks in order to do so.

Equity (Also Known as Owner's or Shareholder's Equity): Equity is the amount of money invested in the company by the owners (shareholders) plus any earnings retained (not paid out to owners) minus any liabilities or any money taken out in the form of draws.

Expenses: Expenses are costs incurred by a business to generate income. Expenses can be fixed (such as rents or salaries) or variable—those that fluctuate depending on sales or production cycles.

Fiscal Year: A fiscal year is the 12-month period that constitutes the start and end of the annual financial records for a business. It does not necessarily correspond to the calendar year. For example, seasonal businesses such as farming often use a fiscal year that ends in the fall.

General Ledger: The general ledger is the complete recording of a company's financial transactions over the lifetime of the organization, including assets, liabilities, revenue, expenses, and equity.

Income: Money received, especially on a regular basis, for work or through investments.

Income Statement: The income statement (also known as a profit and loss statement) shows your revenues, expenses, and profit for a particular period. It's a snapshot of your business that shows whether or not your business is profitable at that point in time. The basic equation of the income statement is: revenue minus expenses equals profit or loss.

Liabilities: Liabilities are financial obligations owed by the company, including salaries, income taxes, rents, utilities, interest payments, and amounts owed to suppliers. Liabilities can be short or long term and are grouped on balance sheets in order of classification.

Marketing: The action or business of promoting and selling products or services, including market research and advertising.

Marketing Mix (4P's of Marketing): Place, Price, Promotion, and Place.

Marketing Plan Strategies: Advertising, Direct marketing, trade shows (all the things that create your favorable business image).

Marketing Research: Drives a better understanding of customer behavior and buying patterns.

Product: An article or substance that is manufactured or refined for sale.

Revenue: A business' gross revenue is the sum of all monies generated through the sale of goods and services, interest charged, royalties, sale of assets, rental property, and more, before subtracting expenses.

Sale: the exchange of a commodity for money; the action of selling something.

Sales Plan: A strategy that sets out sales targets and identifies the steps you will take to meet your targets.

Sell: Give or hand over (something) in exchange for money.

Taxes: A compulsory contribution to state revenue, levied by the government on workers' income and business profits, or added to the cost of some goods, services, and transactions.

Made in the USA
Columbia, SC
23 August 2020